ADAPTATION FOR SURVIVAL

NOSES

WRITTEN BY STEPHEN SAVAGE

Thomson Learning
New York

ADAPTATION FOR SURVIVAL

Books in the series

- EYES • EARS • HANDS AND FEET
- MOUTHS • NOSES • SKIN

Front cover: Piglets; a mother and baby; and two elephants with trunks entwined in battle

Title page: Horses on the Camargue, a river island in France

First published in the United States in 1995 by
Thomson Learning
New York, NY

Published simultaneously in Great Britain by Wayland (Publishers) Limited

U.S. version copyright © 1995 Thomson Learning

U.K. version copyright © 1995 Wayland (Publishers) Limited

Library of Congress Cataloging-in-Publication
Savage, Stephen, 1965–
    Noses / written by Stephen Savage.
        p.   cm.—(Adaptation for survival)
    Includes bibliographical references and index.
    Summary: Points out that noses vary greatly in size, shape,
and ability, and have a range of uses including breathing,
finding food, and warning of danger.
    ISBN 1-56847-354-0 (hc)
    1. Noses—Juvenile literature. 2. Smell—Juvenile literature.
[1. Nose. 2. Smell. 3. Senses and sensation.] I. Title. II. Series:
Savage, Stephen, 1965–   Adaptation for survival.
QL947.S28   1995
591.1'826—dc20   95-19238

Printed in Italy

Picture acknowledgments

The publishers would like to thank the following for allowing their photographs to be reproduced in this book: Ardea London Ltd.: 7 (bottom/Ron & Valerie Taylor), 15 (bottom/Ian Beames), 19 (top/J. Mason), 22 (Roy & Valerie Taylor); Bruce Coleman Ltd.: 4 (Michel Viard), 6 (Roger Coggan), 7 (top/Rod Williams), 12 (top/Erwin & Peggy Bauer) (bottom/Leonard Lee Rue), 13 (Dieter & Mary Plage), 14 (Bob & Clara Calhoun), 17 (top/ Patrick Clement) (bottom/Andrew J. Purcell), 20 (Hans Reinhard), 24 (top/N G Blake), 27 (top) (bottom/Fred Bruemmer), 28 (Adrian Davies), 29 (top/Kim Taylor); Frank Lane Photographic Agency: 23 (bottom/S. Jonasson); Natural History Photographic Agency: *title page* (Henry Ausloos), 9 (ANT), 11 (Peter Johnson), 18 (Nigel J. Dennis), 21 (bottom/Anthony Bannister), 23 (top/David Currey), 25 (top/E. Hanumantha Rao), 29 (bottom/Trevor McDonald); Oxford Scientific Films: *cover* (bottom/Martyn Colbeck), 8 (bottom/Phil Devries), 19 (bottom/Robin Redfern), 24 (bottom/Stan Osolinski), 25 (bottom/David Cayless), 26 (N. A. MacKenzie); Reflections: *cover* (middle/Jennie Woodcock), 21(top/Jennie Woodcock); Stephen Savage 15; Tony Stone Worldwide: 5 (John Wyand); ZEFA: *cover* (top/Larry Lefever), 8 (top), 10 (Frans Lanting), 16. The artwork on pages 4 and 31 is by Peter Bull.

Contents

Human Noses

Although human noses vary in shape and size, they are all used for breathing and smelling. Two nostrils join an airway at the back of the throat and allow air to travel down into the lungs. Small hairs inside the nostrils trap large pieces of dust. This can irritate the nose and cause a sneeze that blows the dust out, keeping it from getting into the lungs and damaging them.

▲ *Humans sometimes use an animal's superior sense of smell to help them in their work. This pig is being used to sniff out truffles (edible fungi that grow underground). Once the pig has shown the man where the truffle is, the man will dig down until he finds it.*

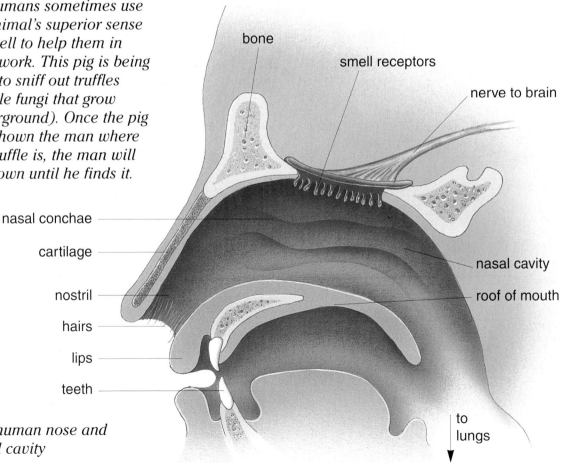

bone

smell receptors

nerve to brain

nasal conchae

cartilage

nostril

hairs

lips

teeth

nasal cavity

roof of mouth

to lungs

The human nose and nasal cavity

Almost everybody can smell strong scents. They will enjoy the fragrance of a particular flower or complain about an unpleasant smell. Some people, however, seem to have very sensitive noses. They are able to use their sense of smell for their work, such as testing perfumes or tasting wines.

By smelling the wine, as well as tasting it, a wine tester can tell if the wine is ready to be put into bottles and sold. People talk about wine having a "bouquet."

An animal's nose and sense of smell are adapted to its needs. Some animals might need to find food that is hidden from sight; others might need to be able to detect danger in time to escape from it. Noses vary greatly in size, shape, and ability, and they are put to a range of uses.

Breathing

All mammals (including humans), reptiles, birds, and some amphibians use their noses for breathing. Although most can breathe through their mouths if they choose to, their noses allow them to breathe while their mouths are closed and while they are eating. The air that is taken in through the nose (or mouth) passes down into the lungs. Here, the oxygen in the air is absorbed into the bloodstream. Like all creatures, without this oxygen humans cannot live, and breathing is therefore the most important thing our bodies do.

Mammals that live in water take in air either through nostrils (for example, seals, otters, and hippopotamuses), or through

A seal's nostrils are closed for most of the time, both in the water and on land and have to be opened for the animal to breathe. The mother Weddell seal in this picture has her nostrils open to take in a breath, but her month-old pup has its nostrils closed.

Breathing in a desert sandstorm can be difficult. This camel has extrathick hairs in its nose to keep the sand from getting down into its lungs.

blowholes (whales and dolphins). Both types of airways have to be closed off when the creature dives beneath the surface of the water to prevent water from getting in.

Birds have nostrils on top of their beaks. These are extremely efficient at taking in air because birds need a great deal of oxygen to give them energy to fly. Insects and some small creatures, such as shellfish, do not have noses. These animals breathe through their skin or through special holes in their bodies.

Fish absorb oxygen not from air, but from water. A fish will take in water through its mouth. The water then passes over gills—many layers of a special kind of skin—which take oxygen from the water.

A fish's gills are protected by flaps of skin (gill covers). When a fish is moving, the water flows through its mouth and across its gills. When a fish stays in one place, it flaps its gill covers to create a good flow of water.

Sniffing Out a Meal

▲ *This cougar is using its well-developed sense of smell to track down prey.*

Humans' senses of smell and taste are very closely linked. This is why a person with a bad cold and a blocked nose who is unable to smell anything will often say that food seems tasteless. People tend to eat only food that smells—as well as tastes—good.

Most people these days don't need to use their sense of smell to find their food, although a particularly appetizing smell wafting out of a restaurant might tempt them in. Most animals, though, do use their sense of smell to find food.

The anteater uses its highly sensitive nose to find termites and ants. Its nose is on the end of a long snout, and the nostrils are protected by thick hairs.

Animals and fish that eat meat, such as wolves, lions, and sharks, will use their sense of smell to find food. A polar bear can smell a seal pup in a birth den up to three feet beneath the snow, and a wolf can smell the scent of its prey from a distance of over a thousand feet.

Nocturnal animals, such as hedgehogs, look for their prey in the dark. They use their noses to help them do this. Moles (which are nearly blind) tunnel through the earth, using their noses to help them find food, such as earthworms. Even animals that eat only plants and fruit use their noses to tell one plant from another or to find out if a fruit is ripe enough to eat.

Some sharks cruise the oceans seeking food. They can use their sensitive noses to detect the smell of blood from injured fish or sea mammals up to 450 yards away.

The Smell of Danger

Many animals, especially those that spend a large part of their time with their heads down, eating, rely on the sense of smell to warn them of danger. Deer and antelope feed mainly on grass and leaves. Every now and then they will lift their heads and sniff the air for any signs of danger. Rabbits will also stop nibbling the grass and stand on their hind legs, turning this way and that to sniff for danger.

These impala are using all their senses, including their sense of smell, to determine whether they are in danger.

Caribou (reindeer) often roam over great distances and are in constant danger of being attacked by wolves. They frequently stop to sniff the air before moving on. European badgers leave the safety of their sets to hunt for food under the cover of darkness. At the slightest smell of danger, the badgers will retreat to safety.

Although humans are usually not aware of their own scents, they are easily detected by other mammals. When watching animals such as foxes or deer, a person must approach them downwind so that the human scent is blown away from the animals.

It is thought that some animals, such as dogs, can smell fear in humans. What they are smelling is almost certainly the scent of the sweat that the human body produces when a person is scared.

The smell of danger will send a herd of fur seals rushing across the beach to the comparative safety of the water.

11

Scent Marking

Many animals mark the borders of their territories with their scent. This scent warns animals of the same kind that the area already belongs to another. Scent marking therefore helps to prevent unnecessary meetings and fights. Some scents also include smells that show if the animal is a male or female and if it is ready to mate.

A pronghorn antelope rubbing its scent onto twigs and grasses from a special gland beneath its eye

▼ *An antelope's urine also contains a scent that will send signals to other animals.*

Animals mark their territory in different ways. Some, such as otters and red foxes, use scented droppings and urine to mark their territory. Others, such as tree shrews, mark their territory with scent from glands on the throat and chest. Male rabbits mark the area around their warrens using scent

This tigress is sniffing the scent markings left by another tiger.

glands beneath their chins. Some small mammals, such as the dwarf mongoose, do a handstand and project their urine high up on a tree or rock so that other animals will think they are larger than they are.

A pet male dog will urinate frequently on posts and trees. In doing this he is leaving his scent so that any other dog will know that he has been there. This behavior is left over from when all dogs were wild. A male house cat marks its territory in a similar way, as do large cats, such as the tiger.

Phew!

Many animals and birds rely on their predators having a sense of smell. They produce an unpleasant smell as a way of defending themselves. The best-known animal for this is the skunk. The skunk's first defense is to raise its tail as a warning. If this doesn't work, it squirts a fine spray of a liquid with an extremely strong smell that might linger for several days.

By the time it is one month old, a skunk is able to spray a strong-smelling liquid at an attacker.

The author, Stephen Savage, showing a group of children a garter snake. Garter snakes can produce a smelly liquid if frightened, so handling them can be tricky.

Minnows (small fish) give off an alarm scent when injured. Although this doesn't help the injured fish, the scent warns other minnows of the danger so that they can avoid the area. Wasps also give off a smell when attacked. If there are other wasps nearby, they will come to the first wasp's aid. This is why it is dangerous to swat at a wasp and make it angry.

Some caterpillars and beetles avoid being eaten by giving off a horrible smell, in the hope that animals will expect them to taste horrible too. Ladybugs can give off a foul-smelling liquid to warn off an attacker. This yellow liquid is actually blood.

Sawfly caterpillars defend themselves from predators by raising their back ends in the air and giving off a foul smell. When attacked by a foraging ant, the sawfly will deposit a smelly gum on the ant's head. This confuses the ant and prevents it from following its own scent trail back to the ant nest and bringing reinforcements.

The fulmar is able to defend itself against animals and birds without even leaving its nest. It simply spits a smelly, oily liquid at anything that comes too close.

Following a Trail

Leaf-cutter ants following a scent trail between their nest and the leaves they are chopping up

As you travel to school or walk around town, you will probably notice a variety of smells. You may detect the smell of bread from a bakery, a fragrant bush in a garden, the smell of the chemicals used by a dry cleaner, or the smell of a pig farm or factory. But would you be able to use these smells to find your way around? Probably not, but this is what some animals do.

Salmon have a spectacular sense of smell. They spend much of their adult lives at sea, traveling thousands of miles, but return to the rivers in which they themselves hatched in order to lay their own eggs. It would seem that a salmon finds its birth river by its distinctive smell.

Mice leave scent trails along routes they use so that they can find their way back to safety.

The nocturnal galago solves the problem of how to find its way home in the dark by urinating on its paws before it sets out. The urine leaves a scent trail on the branches it clings to so that the galago can return along the same route.

Dogs have a particularly good sense of smell and are frequently used by humans to help them follow trails. Dogs have been used by humans to help them hunt animals for food and sport for thousands of years. More recently, dogs have been trained to find people buried in the rubble of buildings after earthquakes.

▼ *Common frogs return to water each year to lay their eggs. They find their way to a suitable pond by detecting the odor given off by algae that form in still water at a certain time of year. The tadpoles that hatch from the frogs' eggs will feed on the algae.*

Group Living

Scents and smells are important for animals that live in groups. Animals need to be able to leave the group to hunt or forage for food and to be accepted by the rest of the animals in the group when they return. An animal's distinctive smell tells another animal of the same kind whether the approaching animal belongs to the group or is an outsider that must be turned away.

Dwarf mongooses live in large groups. They all take their dust baths in the same spot, so they take on each other's smell and develop a sort of group scent.

Some animals that live in groups share their scents. Lions regularly rub their heads against each other, passing their scents on to other members of the pride. This creates a group smell, although each lion's own scent is also still present. When a pet cat rubs its head against its owner, it is also passing on its scent, making its owner one of its family group.

Many humans try hard to cover up their bodies' natural scent signals. They put on artificial scents in the form of perfumes and deodorants.

▲ Some bees have a communal scent, so bees returning to the hive can be identified as belonging to it. The group scent changes over time, so if a bee spends too long away from the hive, its "scent label" becomes out of date. If it tries to return, it risks being killed by the other bees.

When meeting another member of its group, a European badger will pass its scent on to the other badger's body.

Mothers and Babies

Smell is a very important way for a young animal to recognize its mother and for a mother to recognize her offspring. When a mother antelope or cow licks her newborn calf clean, she is also learning to identify the calf's scent. At the same time, the calf is learning the scent of its mother.

A mother sheep gets to know the smell of her lamb and will allow only her own lamb to feed from her.

It is important that a young animal not be separated from its mother before this scent bond is formed. If this happens, the mother will not recognize her offspring and will not feed or look after it. Similarly, if a foreign smell is introduced by a human that handles the baby, the mother may also reject it. A mother tree shrew actually marks her young with her own scent so that she will recognize them.

▲ *A human mother and baby soon learn each other's scent, although human mothers tend not to find their babies by following their noses!*

It is important for the mother seal to get to know her pup's scent as soon as it is born in case it is separated from her on the crowded breeding grounds.

This ability to recognize scent is especially important in animals that give birth on breeding grounds. A mother sea lion will give birth to her pup among hundreds of other sea lions. The mother then has to leave her pup on the beach so that she can feed at sea. When she returns, she will first find her pup by its call and then makes sure it is hers by checking its scent.

Underwater

Although fish take in oxygen from the water that passes across their gills, they also have nostrils. They use their nostrils to smell and track down food.

Other creatures that live in the sea, such as dolphins and whales, have to come to the surface to breathe in air. These sea mammals have a kind of nostril known as a blowhole on top of their heads.

Fish have a pair of nostrils on each side of their heads. As they move forward, water flows into one hole and is forced out the other. Their smell receptor cells detect the scent of food (or danger) in the water.

As a whale surfaces, it opens its blowhole and blows out stale air (which has had the oxygen taken out of it in the whale's lungs). The whale then quickly takes another breath and closes its blowhole before disappearing beneath the waves. Some whales have one blowhole and some have two.

Neither dolphins nor whales have a sense of smell. Seals cannot use their sense of smell in the sea because they have to close their nostrils to keep water from getting in, but they do have a sense of smell on land.

▲ *A gray whale blowing air out of its blowholes.*

If this gannet had nostrils like those of mammals or most other birds, water would shoot up its nose when it dove into the water. Instead, its nostrils have been closed off by a piece of bone, and the gannet breathes through a flap on its beak.

Supernose

▲ *The end of an elephant's trunk is specially adapted for grasping food.*

An elephant has a very long nose called a trunk. The elephant uses it for all sorts of different things. Like most mammals, the elephant breathes through its nose and smells things with it. It also uses it to reach leaves from high branches or to pull up grass. The elephant grasps food with the end of its trunk and passes the food to its mouth. It can also drink with its nose, as shown below.

An elephant drinks by sucking up water into its trunk and squirting it into its mouth.

Elephants also suck up water to give themselves, or each other, a shower. Afterward, they pick up dirt and throw it over themselves to protect their skin from insect bites. An elephant may even pick up a stick in its trunk and use it to scratch an itch.

Elephants greet other members of their herd by touching and stroking them with their trunks. An elephant may wave its trunk or throw dust in the air as a warning to an intruder.

Having a long nose is particularly useful when swimming. This baby elephant is using its trunk like a snorkel.

▲ *Indian elephants are used by humans to perform heavy tasks. This elephant is making use of its trunk (and tusks) to carry a log.*

Nose Talk

A few animals actually "talk" through their noses. Apart from the many uses an elephant has for its trunk, it can also use it to make trumpeting sounds. Elephants living together in a group keep in touch with each other by making noises. They fall silent only if danger is near. They will raise their trunks in the air to threaten possible predators or competitors.

The elephant seal, with a nose like a shortened trunk, uses its nose to amplify (make louder) the honking sound it produces. The male proboscis monkey also makes a loud honking sound through its nose to warn others of possible danger.

A male proboscis monkey in Southeast Asia. The size of its nose indicates how important it is in the social group. All the older males have large droopy noses, but the most important, the dominant male, has the largest nose of all. (Female proboscis monkeys have relatively small noses.)

Some of the sounds dolphins and whales make come from the blowholes on top of their heads. These sounds are made above water or just below the surface and are probably used to pass information to one another, although humans cannot understand their language.

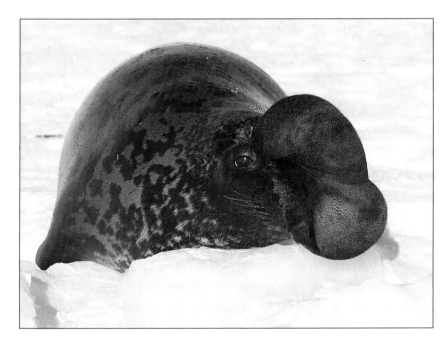

The hooded seal makes good use of its large nose. It can inflate its whole nose by closing its nostrils and blowing.

▼ *By closing one nostril and blowing air into the hood, the hooded seal can also blow a large balloon of skin through the other nostril. It does either of these things as a warning or when it gets excited.*

Where Is My Nose?

This male emperor moth uses its fernlike antennae to detect the scent of a female moth.

Some animals do not actually have what are called noses, but they are still able to detect smells. Insects, shrimp, and lobsters have special antennae that stick up from their heads. They feel, taste, and smell things with them. The male silkworm moth has large fern-like antennae that can detect the scent of a female from three miles away.

As with mammals that live in groups, insects that live in colonies have group smells. They can recognize other members of their group and quickly detect intruders. Ants use their antennae to taste, smell, and touch things. When attacked, they give off a warning smell that attracts the aid of other ants.

In the sea, cockles live buried in the sand. They do not need smell to find food, which they can filter from the water through a breathing tube. They can, however, smell an approaching starfish, which is one of their main predators. The cockle flips itself along the seabed, using its single foot to escape its attacker.

Mosquitoes use their antennae to detect the scent of carbon dioxide in the breath of animals, including humans.

Whelks have special cells in their breathing tubes that detect the smell of food, such as a dead crab or fish. They move the tube around to find the strongest smell and then set out in search of the source.

Glossary

Amphibians Cold-blooded animals that live both on land and in the water.

Antennae Feelers on the heads of animals such as insects or lobsters.

Appetizing Looks and smells good to eat.

Artificial Made by humans; not occurring naturally.

Breeding grounds A place where many animals of the same species give birth or hatch out their eggs.

Extract Take out of.

Forage Search for food.

Fragrance Pleasant scent.

Gills The part of the fish that transfers oxygen from the water into the fish's blood. The gills are found in gill slits, or gill covers, on either side of the fish's head and consist of many flaps of a special kind of skin, called membrane, that is full of blood vessels.

Inflate To make bigger by filling with air.

Nocturnal Sleeping by day and active by night.

Odor A scent.

Oxygen A gas that is present in the air and is necessary for all animals to live.

Predator An animal that hunts other animals.

Prey An animal that is hunted.

Reptiles Cold-blooded animals that take oxygen from the air.

Scent gland A part of the body that makes and gives out a smelly substance.

Set The burrow of a badger.

Warren The network of tunnels lived in by rabbits.

Further Reading

Bennett, Paul. *Catching a Meal.* Nature's Secrets. New York: Thomson Learning, 1994.

Parker, Steve. *Touch, Taste and Smell.* The Human Body. Revised edition. New York: Franklin Watts, 1989.

Wright, Lillian. *Smelling and Tasting.* First Starts Health Series. Milwaukee: Raintree Steck-Vaughn, 1994.

Further notes

Humans have five senses, each of which contributes to their awareness of their environment, thereby helping them to survive. All animals experience the world through a combination of senses. Scents are very important in the lives of many animals—as a way of finding food, avoiding danger, and of communicating. Although humans try to cover up their natural smells, these scents may have a greater effect on our lives than people think.

Breathing

As a person breathes, air is drawn in through the nostrils. Hairs trap particles of dust that would otherwise damage the lungs. Even smaller particles are trapped by microscopic hairs and mucus produced by special cells in the nasal lining. Water that is drained away from the eyeball enters the nasal cavity.

Smell

Smell travels through the air in the form of thousands of tiny, invisible particles, almost like an invisible dust. The particles of scent are breathed into the nose. The smell is detected by the small receptors in the lining of the roof of the nose and a message is sent to the brain via the olfactory nerve. These smells are analyzed by the brain and matched with smells already experienced.

Some substances, such as sugary water, have almost no smell to humans. To animals such as wasps, however, sugar water may smell as strong as gasoline does to humans.

Parts of the human nose

Nostrils – Two passages that allow air into the nose for breathing and smelling.

Cartilage – Substance like bone, but more flexible.

Nasal cavity – A hollow chamber inside the nose, lined with microscopic hairs (cilia) and mucus-secreting cells (the mucous membrane) that trap small particles of dust.

Smell receptors – Special cells that detect smell.

Olfactory nerve – Sends messages about smell to the brain.

Hair – Traps dust and dirt and keeps it from being breathed into the lungs.

Nasal conchae – Shelflike bones that project inward and increase the area of the nasal lining.

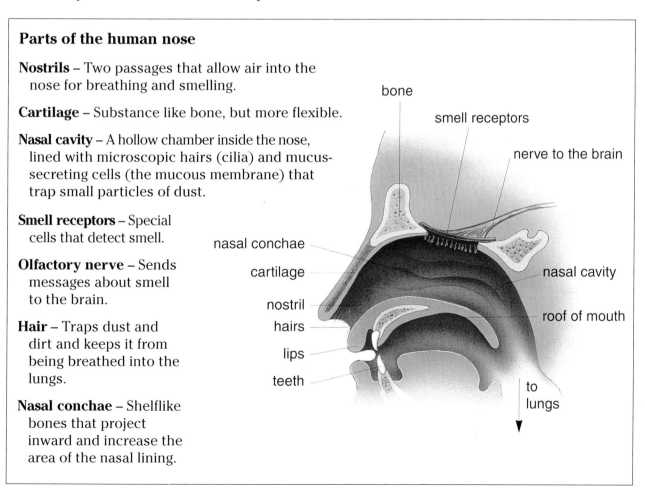

bone

smell receptors

nerve to the brain

nasal conchae

cartilage

nostril

hairs

lips

teeth

nasal cavity

roof of mouth

to lungs

Index